TEACH THEM YOUNG

ABC'S

African American Edition

Shamariah Starr

For permissions and information:
Esther Lewis
shamariahstarrsocial@gmail.com
Instagram: @shamariahstarr

Illustrator: Arnav Chakraborty

ISBN 978-0-5789-9385-0 (hardcover)
ISBN 979-8-2180-7165-3 (paperback)
ISBN 979-8-2180-7166-0 (ebook)

Printed in the United States of America.

DeDication

Thanks be to God! And thank you mom and dad
for your constant unwavering support.
Love you guys!

LET'S LEARN OUR ABC'S!

A is for Africa

Our native land. Where it all began.

B is for BRILLIANT

We are all brilliant in our own unique ways.

C is for cookout

A gathering outside with music, family, friends, and BBQ.

D is for DOUBLE DUTCH

A fun jump rope game we play outside.

E is for entrepreneurs

We own
successful
businesses.

F is for FAITH

FAITH

HIS EYE IS ON THE SPARROW

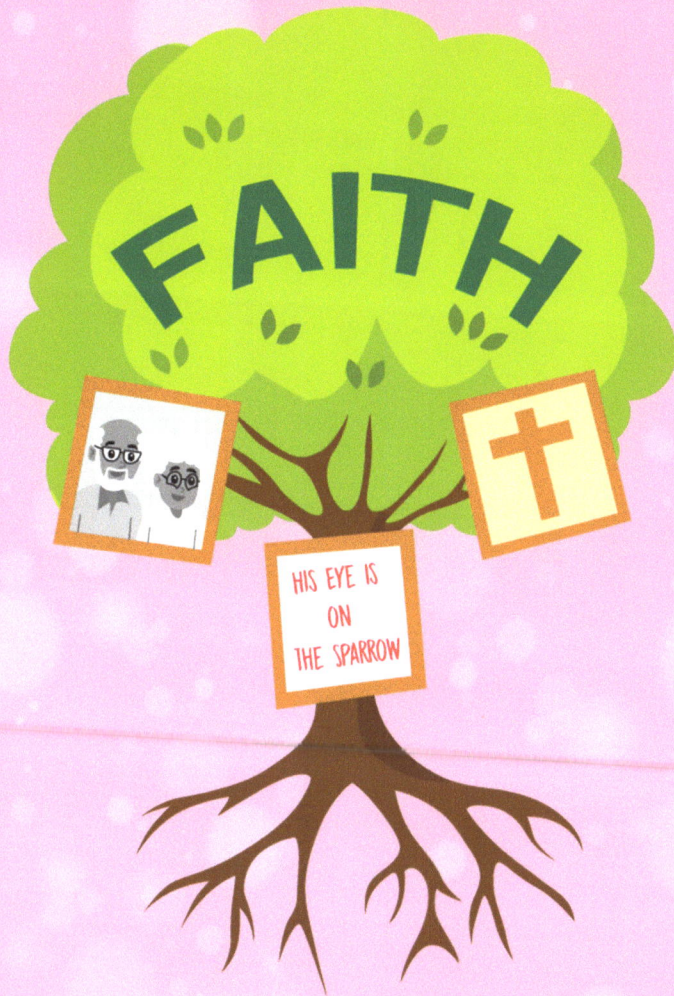

We stand strong and tall through faith.

G is for GIVING

We are kind and generous.

H is for HBCUS

HBCUs

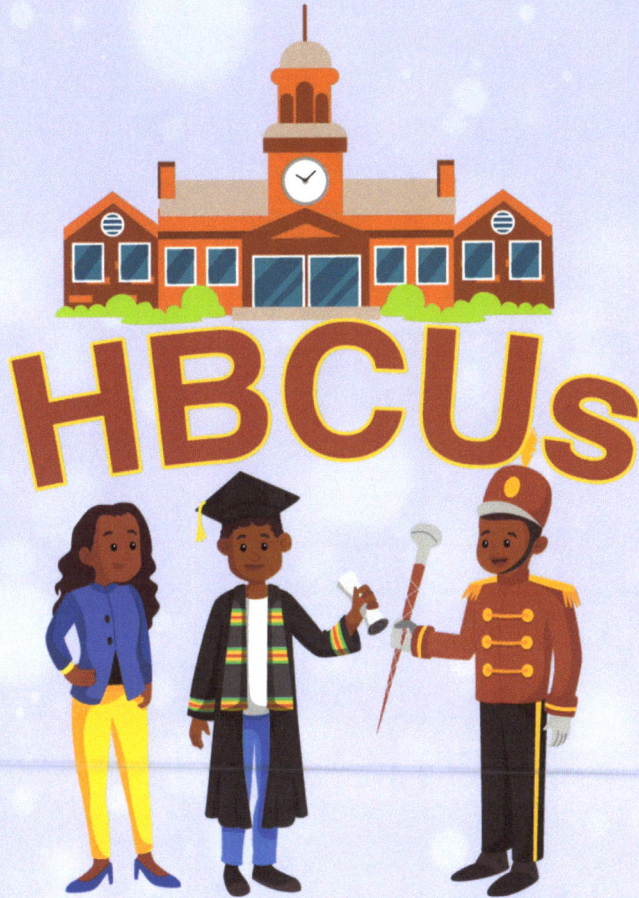

Where sisterhoods and brotherhoods are formed.

I is for INNOVATION

Innovation

We invented the first wooden clock and traffic light.

J is for JAZZ

A genre of music we created.

K is for KINGS

We are powerful Kings.

L is for LEADERS

We lead by
example.
We make wise
decisions.

M is for MARTIN & MALCOM

Civil rights leaders who fought for our freedom.

N is for NATURAL

We love our natural hair. Our kinks, curls, coils, and naps are awesome!

O is for ORGAN

A musical instrument used
mostly in Church.

P is for PROUD

SAY IT
LOUD!
I'M
BLACK
AND I'M
PROUD!

We are proud of our diverse
and vibrant community.

Q is for QUEENS

We are
dynamic
queens.

R is for RESILIENT

We defy all
odds. We are
victorious.

S is for SOUL FOOD

Yummy food from the deep south.

T is for Tulsa

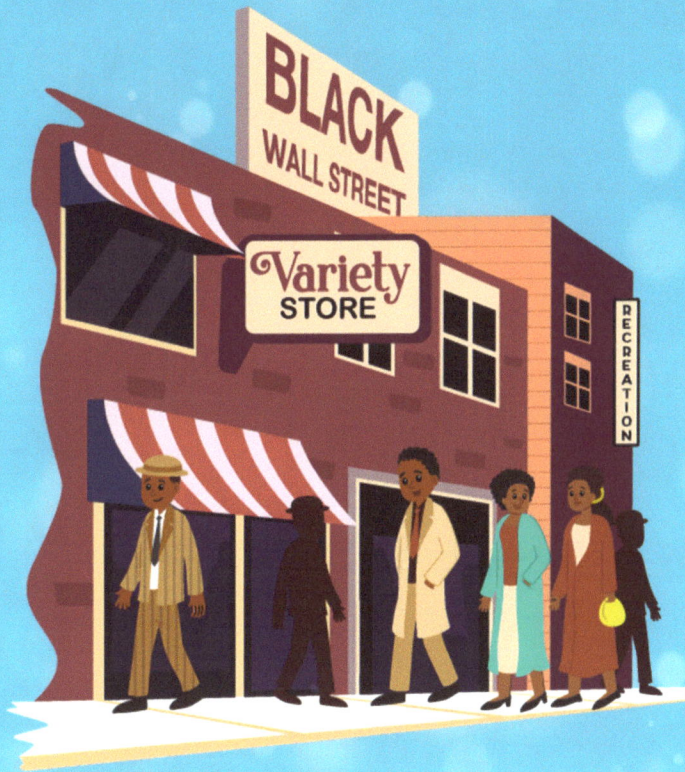

Black Wall Street. A once thriving black community.

U is for UNITED

We work together, hand in hand, for a better future.

V is for VERSATILE

We are talented and can learn any skill.

W is for WAKANDA

WAKANDA

An imaginary society that
we hope to create one day.

X is for xai-xai

A beautiful tourist city in Mozambique, Africa.

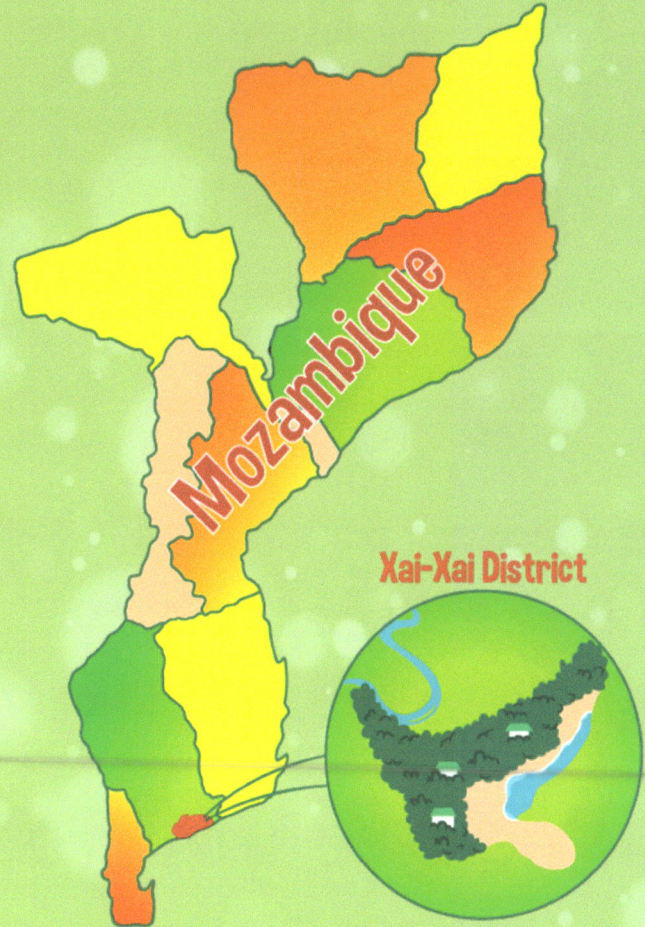

Mozambique

Xai-Xai District

Y is for YOUTH

We are young and creative.

Z is for ZILLIONS

There are many of us cheering you on!

TEACH THEM YOUNG

ABC'S BOOK Activities

Find the hidden words that are listed
Words can be up down diagonal or forword

```
Q I K E L V S U Y Z N C N M A E U
E G V F N N H A F V G P D M T R D
Y N T X R B C L U N E L L M C K K
X O N B L V B L E S S E D H V D H
X R N V C M E L E A D E R S H N N
C T E U K X L G W B P R S G K T T L
V S B U T Z P G W Z N L V E S O X
S A I P W C R I W E S R G F V S E
K M G R K F O J E S B X P E D Q F
I I H K P P Z U O Z Q C D S W K U
M Z F R E H Q E U H A S Z W S U C
X K M N L D B G F M E E C O M Y X
L B O V L O P E L S E U L P A D O
I Q J O I N O X G Y Q J O X R A J
P K B Q M U H E P E J I G D T D X
K N W G B O V X B Q V I Q P S F K
T G Z W O F U O Y F Q D X C K A X
```

QUEENS   SMART   LEADERS   BLESSED

LOVED   BOLD   STRONG

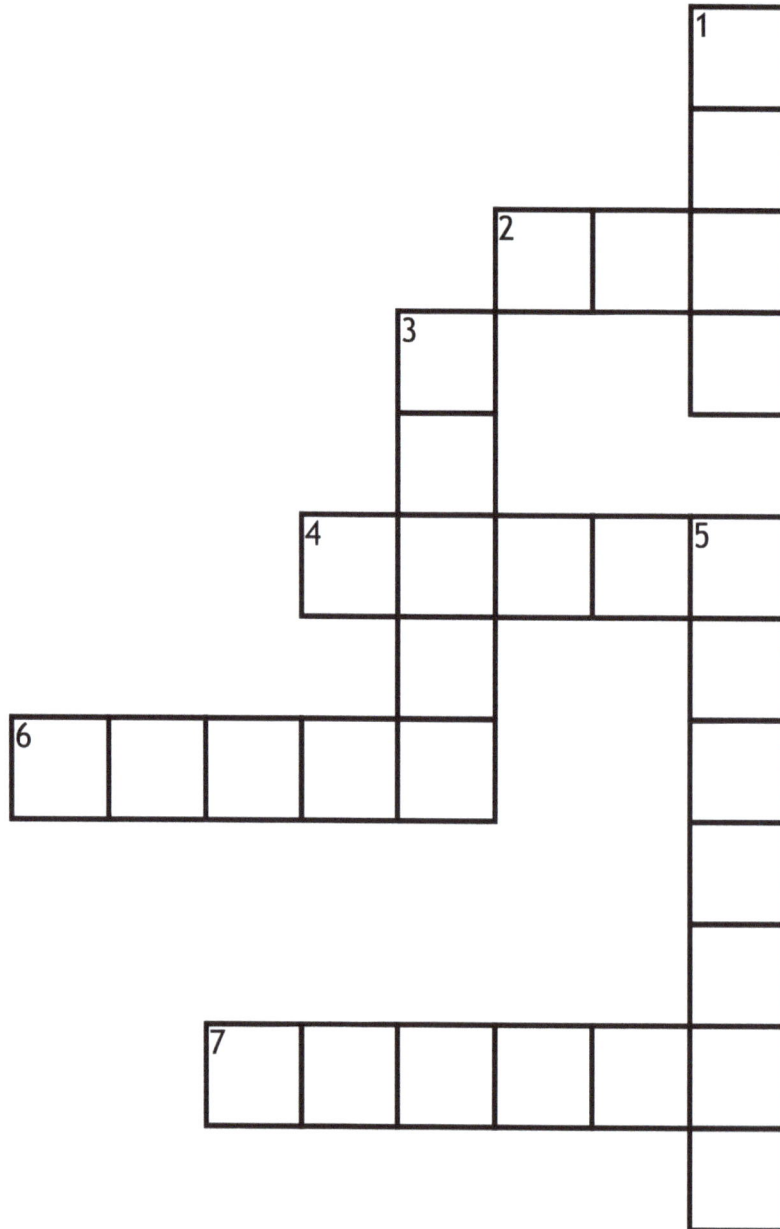

Solve the Crossword Puzzle

Across
2. FUN
4. KINGS
6. YOUTH
7. AFRICA

Down
1. KIND
3. FAITH
5. SPECIAL

Connect the Dots and Color It

Solve the Maze

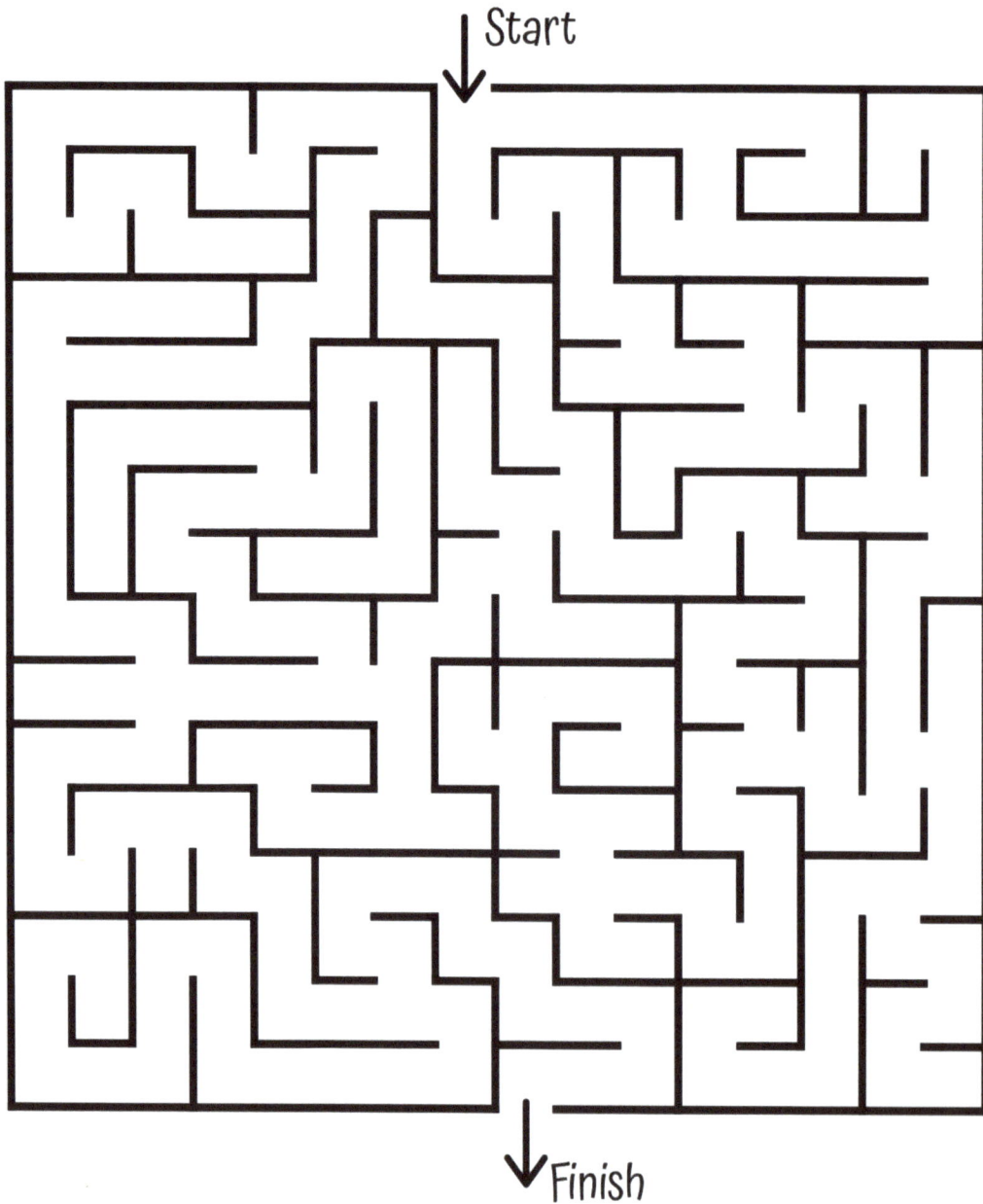

Color the Chocolate according to the Color Code

1. Red   2. Brown   3. Gray

www.ingramcontent.com/pod-product-compliance
Lightning Source LLC
Chambersburg PA
CBHW042010090426

42811CB00015B/1600